WILDKRATTS®
THE OFFICIAL CREATURE POWER GAMES!

DISCOVER THE FASTEST, STRONGEST, FIERCEST, BIGGEST AND TINIEST ANIMALS ON THE PLANET

ADVENTURE AWAITS!

Time to leap into action! In the following pages, we'll travel all across the world to learn about amazing animals that fly, swim, run, dig and much more! For every creature you meet, there will also be an awesome activity to complete! So grab your thinking cap and get ready, the Creature Power Games are about to begin!

All aboard!

Next stop: fun!

FANTASTIC FLYERS
4 Martial Eagle
6 Canada Goose
8 Carolina Flying Squirrel
10 Pelican
12 Hummingbird
14 Puffin
16 Resplendent Quetzal
18 American Kestrel
20 Dragonfly
22 Black-Capped Chickadee
24 Peacock
26 Loggerhead Shrike
27 Raven
28 Monarch Butterfly
30 Elf Owl
32 Snowy Owl
34 Honey Bee
36 Superb Bird-of-Paradise
38 Golden Eagle
40 Fig Wasp
42 Fruit Fly
44 Purple Martin
46 Luna Moth
47 Caribbean Flamingo

SPECTACULAR SWIMMERS

48 Dragonfish
50 Giant Pacific Octopus
52 Electric Eel
54 Beaver
56 Sockeye Salmon
58 Bowhead Whale
60 Sea Otter
62 Great White Shark
64 Bull Shark
66 Platypus
68 Sea Urchin
70 Blue Marlin
72 Krill
74 Flounder
75 Brine Shrimp
76 Dog-Faced
   Water Snake
78 Giant Manta Ray
80 Red Snapper
82 Humpback Whale
84 Pacific Walrus
86 Loggerhead
   Sea Turtle
88 Salmon Shark

INCREDIBLE LAND-DWELLERS

90 Orangutan
92 Leafcutter Ant
94 African Wildcat
96 Gray Wolf
98 Lion
100 Fossa
102 Honey Badger
104 Domestic Pig
106 African Wild Dog
108 Dwarf Gecko
110 African Elephant
112 Bengal Tiger
114 Howler Monkey
116 European Hedgehog
117 Sambar Deer
118 Ostrich
120 Indian Leopard
122 Egyptian Cobra
124 Koala
126 Giant Panda
128 Giraffe
130 Ermine
132 Komodo Dragon
134 Green Iguana
135 Anole Lizard

GROUNDBREAKING BURROWERS

136 Aardvark
138 River Otter
140 Prairie Dog
142 Lowland
   Streaked Tenrec
144 Clam
146 Bush Dog
148 Vole
150 Sand Cat
152 American
   Alligator
154 Pangolin
156 Norway Lemming
158 Goliath Tarantula
159 Red Fox
160 Aardwolf
162 Warthog
164 Wolverine
166 Indian Crested
   Porcupine
168 Harvester Termite
170 Burrowing Owl
172 Green Anaconda
174 Earthworm

Race ya there!

PLUS! PUZZLES, MAZES AND MANY MORE ACTIVITIES!

MARTIAL EAGLE

Weighing up to 14 pounds with a wingspan of 6 to 8 feet, the martial eagle is the largest eagle in Africa! Not only is she massive, she also has incredible eyesight! With her Creature Power of Spy Vision, the martial eagle can spot prey, such as antelope, snakes, lizards and other birds, from about 3 miles away!

SPY FROM THE SKY

Use Spy Vision like the martial eagle to spot and circle six snakes!

4

Answers on pg. 176

CANADA GOOSE

This goose is quite a traveler! Flying within flocks that make a "V" formation in the sky, the Canada goose migrates south in the colder seasons and north in the warmer seasons. When he gets hungry, he can use his Creature Power of Razor Beak to easily tear vegetation from roots and branches!

In just one day, a Canada goose and his flock can cover about 1,500 miles!

Awesome! I need to book a flight with him!

GOOSE CROSSING

Use the clues below to complete this crossword relating to the Canada goose.

ACROSS

2. A Canada goose flock _____ in a "V" formation.
3. The Canada goose migrates north and _____.
4. The Canada goose uses his _____ to tear vegetation.

DOWN

1. A Canada goose can cover 1,500 _____ in one day.
2. The Canada goose travels with his _____.

Answers on pg. 176

CAROLINA FLYING SQUIRREL

Look at this squirrel soar! Found in the treetops of North America, this guy has a furry membrane that extends from his wrists to his ankles, called a patagium. Using his Creature Power of Super Cape, the Carolina flying squirrel spreads his patagium to glide for great distances to the ground or other trees!

Predators must have a hard time catching this guy!

Yeah, bro! And to be extra safe, the Carolina flying squirrel sleeps during the day and searches for food at night to avoid hungry hunters such as hawks, weasels and coyotes.

SQUIRREL SCRAMBLE

Can you unscramble these words relating to the Carolina flying squirrel?

SERTEPTO _____   PTAAUIMG _____

UFYRR _____   LIGFNY _____

BMMEERAN _____   IDGEL _____

Answers on pg. 176

PELICAN

This guy has one of the biggest bills of all birds! Attached to the pelican's bill is his signature throat pouch, which he uses like a net to catch prey such as fish, crustaceans, turtles and other birds. Once he sees a snack, he uses his Creature Power of Hungry Plunge to dive more than 60 feet into the water!

MENU MATCHING

Find and circle the list that features the pelican's favorite prey!

1
Fish
Frogs
Spiders
Crustaceans

2
Fish
Birds
Turtles
Sandshrews

3
Fish
Crustaceans
Turtles
Birds

4
Fish
Scorpions
Leopard Seals
Turtles

Answers on pg. 176

HUMMINGBIRD

Good luck keeping up with this little bird! With her incredible Creature Power of Whizzing Wings, the hummingbird can fly at 35 to 45 miles per hour for several hours without stopping! Since she is so small and light, the hummingbird sometimes uses wind currents to help save on energy.

HIDING BIRDS

Can you find the five hummingbirds in this scene?

Answers on pg. 176

PUFFIN

Sometimes called a "sea parrot" due to her colorful, triangular beak, this bird is great at both swimming and flying! Underwater, she uses her webbed feet to steer and her strong wings to swim. When it's time to take flight to a new area, the puffin uses her Creature Power of Wonder Wings to flap her wings about 400 times per minute!

SKY AND SEA SEARCH

Can you track down these words relating to the puffin?

SEA PARROT
WINGS
BIRD
UNDERWATER
SWIMMING
FLYING
BEAK
SPRINGTIME
SWIM
FLAP

Answers on pg. 176

O Z W Z P F Y S H P
F I L I Z L O W L L
S P R I N G T I M E
F L A P O G K M K B
C U H Y O K S R B I
U N D E R W A T E R
S W I M M I N G A D
M F U Z T M E F K X
X S E A P A R R O T
X W F L Y I N G S I

RESPLENDENT QUETZAL

The resplendent quetzal is just as splendid as his name suggests! The male quetzal's green upper tail feathers can reach about 3 feet in length—that's almost three times the length of his body from his bill to the base of his tail! During mating season, he uses his Creature Power of Feather Extender to grow longer tail feathers that will attract a mate!

This bird is a great hunter! When searching for food, the resplendent quetzal can swoop down and grasp prey or fruit and then swallow it whole while in the air! Now that's taking your food to go!

QUETZAL QUIZ

Can you answer these questions about the resplendent quetzal?

1. What color are the resplendent quetzal's upper tail feathers?
A. Purple
B. Red
C. Green
D. Pink

2. Thanks to his great hunting skills, how does this bird typically eat his meals?
A. Swallowing them whole in midair
B. Group hunting with other quetzals
C. Grazing while walking on the ground
D. Catching crumbs dropped by other birds

3. Why does the resplendent quetzal grow longer tail feathers?
A. To defend against predators
B. To shield himself from wind
C. To fly faster
D. To attract a mate

4. About how long are this bird's upper tail feathers?
A. 8 feet
B. 3 feet
C. 2 feet
D. 6 feet

Answers on pg. 177

AMERICAN KESTREL

This is the smallest falcon in North America! And thanks to the two eye streaks on each side of her face, she's also one of the most recognizable falcons. When it's dinner time, the American kestrel can dive down to catch ground prey such as scorpions, spiders and mice. Or. she can use her Creature Power of In-Flight Meal to catch flying creatures such as butterflies, moths and dragonflies in midair!

EYE TO THE SKY

Can you find the five American kestrels in this scene?

Answers on pg. 177

DRAGONFLY

Believe it or not, this flying insect's life begins underwater! The dragonfly's larval stage is spent eating tadpoles and small fish until she is ready to emerge from the water. The exoskeleton then splits, and the adult emerges. Before taking her first flight, the adult dries and hardens her wings and legs. Then, she can use her Creature Power of Helicopter Mode to hover, fly up and down or even catch prey in midair!

Whoa, baby! I mean "adult"!

DRAGONFLY JUMBLE

Can you unscramble these words
relating to the dragonfly?

GNSWI _____

TINCES _____

RAVLLA _____

TROPELIEHC _____

KXTOEEOESLN _____

OREVH _____

Answers on pg. 177

The dragonfly
eats so many flying
insects like flies and
mosquitoes, she's actually
a big help in keeping those
populations from getting
out of hand. Thanks for
all the good work
you're doing, my
flying friend!

BLACK-CAPPED CHICKADEE

This creature is well-equipped for the frigid winters of North America. The black-capped chickadee has an amazing memory, which allows him to keep track of hundreds of food items such as berries and seeds that he can gather as needed. To fight off the cold, he uses his Creature Power of Wing Warmth to flap his wings, which beat at a rate of 27 times per second, and fluff up his feathers to trap warm air close to his body!

Wow, winter weather is no match for this guy!

That's right, bro! And aside from the weather, this guy also has to keep himself safe from predators such as hawks, owls and squirrels. Fortunately, he communicates with other chickadees through special calls, which can be used as danger warnings!

EYE TO THE SKY

Can you find the five black-capped chickadees in this scene?

Answers on pg. 177

PEACOCK

This guy certainly stands out in a crowd! The peacock is known for the bright, colorful covert feathers on his tail, which can grow up to 5 feet long! Even though his collection of feathers is bigger than his body, this guy can still fly. He forages for food on the ground during the day, but when the sun sets, he uses his Creature Power of Night Flight to soar up into the trees away from potential predators!

What a super cool-looking bird!

SPOT THE DIFFERENCE

Can you find and circle the five differences between these two peacocks?

Answers on pg. 177

You said it, bro! The name "peacock" only refers to the males—these birds are called peafowl collectively, while females are called peahens and babies are called peachicks!

LOGGERHEAD SHRIKE

He may look harmless, but this bird is fierce! The loggerhead shrike perches at the top of a tree watching for prey such as snakes, mice and insects. When he spots something tasty, he uses his Creature Power of Tackle Attack to swoop down and pounce!

The loggerhead shrike lacks the big talons necessary for grasping and tearing food, but he has a smart solution for this. This bird has learned to impale his prey on thorns and branches, similar to the way we eat food with a fork!

PREY WATCH

Help the loggerhead shrike spot the following creatures from his perch:

1 snake   4 insects

26

Answers on pg. 177

RAVEN

This is one smart bird! Typically found in a flock, the raven makes good use of having her friends around. Using her Creature Power of Teamwork Tactics, she works together with her flock to take down larger prey or even to distract other birds while another raven steals eggs from a nest! Perhaps this coordinated sneakery is why a flock of ravens is called a conspiracy!

As for the raven's own nest, she can get pretty creative when it comes to building materials. She can weave together sticks, sheep's wool and even different man-made materials she finds to make a very sturdy nest for her eggs. Maybe I could get her to make me a tree fort sometime!

BIRD SEARCH

Can you find these words relating to the raven?

CONSPIRACY	EGGS	PREY
FLOCK	WOOL	WEAVE
NEST	TEAMWORK	STICKS
	TACTICS	

```
T  W  R  I  W  G  K  C  R  M
W  A  S  E  O  N  Q  O  E  J
P  E  C  H  O  C  B  N  G  T
R  O  A  T  L  H  Y  S  G  E
E  F  F  V  I  G  J  P  S  A
Y  O  L  N  E  C  G  I  T  M
J  L  B  O  B  X  S  R  I  W
V  M  E  G  C  G  H  A  C  O
N  E  S  T  J  K  S  C  K  R
A  O  H  M  Q  I  M  Y  S  K
```

Answers on pg. 178

MONARCH BUTTERFLY

Meet the amazing monarch! As the weather gets colder, this beautiful butterfly uses her Creature Power of Mighty Migration to fly across North America, either south or southwest, to areas with warmer climates! This process involves the monarch riding strong winds to save energy and using her internal compass and the sun's position to determine the direction she needs to go!

That's a lot of intelligence packed into a tiny brain!

Absolutely, and that's not all! The monarch butterfly's bright coloring isn't just pretty, it's a warning to predators that she doesn't taste good! Because of the milkweed she ate as a caterpillar, her body is filled with the toxins found in that plant. If eaten, she could cause harm to her predators that can't eat milkweed!

MIGRATION MAZE

Can you help the monarch butterfly fly south to her migration destination?

Answer on pg. 178

END

ELF OWL

Even though he's the smallest owl species in North America, the elf owl is one skilled hunter. Thanks to his excellent hearing, he's able to hunt in complete darkness by simply listening for his prey, which includes the likes of crickets, scorpions, centipedes and beetles. Once he hears a potential meal, he uses his Creature Power of Silent Flight to swoop down and catch it without making a sound!

ODD OWL OUT

Can you find the elf owl that doesn't look like the others?

Answer on pg. 178

SNOWY OWL

It's no secret how this beautiful bird got her name—she's as white as the snow that surrounds her! Unlike other owl species, the snowy owl mostly hunts during the day, perching on the ground or on short posts to await her next meal. When prey are beneath the snow or difficult to spot, the snowy owl uses her Creature Power of Ultra Hearing to sense the likes of lemmings, birds, fish and rabbits she can catch for dinner!

Incoming!

SNOWY SEARCH

Use your best searching skills to find these words related to the snowy owl!

ARCTIC

EYES

PERCH

FEATHERS

FLY

LEMMINGS

BIRDS

FISH

RABBITS

WHITE

Answers on pg. 178

```
N F N D K K I M S Y
F E A T H E R S P I
M A A R C T I C X Z
F W Y U A R A G W X
L H F Q N B I R D S
Y I I E Z V B F Q H
Y T V E Y E S I G E
L E M M I N G S T M
W Y R M C X T H H S
P E R C H A S N W R
```

Even though her preferred hunting time is different, the snowy owl is still like other owls when it comes to catching her prey. When she's on the hunt, she flies low to the ground and uses big, sharp talons on her feet to snatch up her snack!

HONEY BEE

This insect is un-bee-lievable! While the honey bee does go through several development stages, the whole process from a little white egg to the fuzzy, busy bee you see on flowers only takes about 21 days! Honey bees live in hives in an organized group called a colony, which has a queen, workers and drones. When a worker honey bee is old enough, she can use her Creature Power of Buzzy Business Trip to fly outside the hive in search of a good food source or a location for a new home!

Honey bees survive the cold winter season by eating the honey they made during the spring, summer and fall. That's pretty impressive—I would be eating that sweet, sticky stuff all year round!

JUMBLE BEE

Can you unscramble these words relating to the honey bee?

OOLYCN_____

ORRWKE_____

IHEV_____

LFY_____

OHYNE_____

ZFYZU_____

WLEFRO_____

Answers on pg. 178

hat fancy name isn't just for fun—this bird has earned his title! Native to the rainforests of New Guinea, the superb bird-of-paradise basically transforms himself into a big, dancing smiley face when he sees a female: Using his Creature Power of Dance Break, he spreads out his long neck feathers like a cape, lifts his crown to show off his bright eye-like markings and exposes his shiny blue breast feathers!

SUPERB BIRD WORDS

Can you find these words relating to the superb bird-of-paradise?

RAINFOREST   NEW GUINEA
DANCE   MARKINGS
HOP   CAPE
FEATHERS   TRANSFORMS
CROWN   BLUE

```
O I F E A T H E R S
C N E W G U I N E A
T R A N S F O R M S
H B C D C R O W N T
O L A Y A W V F A S
P U P M Z N E D K H
L E E C H J C K E J
R A I N F O R E S T
S J M A R K I N G S
I Y O A N O M J Q J
```

Answers on pg. 178

GOLDEN EAGLE

Check out this big bird! The golden eagle stands between 2½ and 3 feet tall, weighs up to 14 pounds and has a giant wingspan ranging between 6 and 7½ feet! When it's time to hunt prey such as rabbits, squirrels, reptiles and fish, she swoops down and uses her Creature Power of Talon Attack to snatch up her meal!

Even before she latches onto her prey with those big talons on her feet, the golden eagle shows off another amazing hunting skill. When she dives from the sky, this bird of prey can reach speeds of more than 150 miles per hour!

Wow, she must get a speeding ticket every time she finds a meal!

CROSSBIRD PUZZLE

Use the clues below to complete this crossword relating to the golden eagle!

ACROSS

2. Aquatic prey
5. Hunting action that allows speeds exceeding 150 miles per hour
6. Prey that hops
7. Scaly, cold-blooded prey found on land and in water
8. Ranges between 6 and 7.5 feet

DOWN

1. Used to snatch up prey
3. Prey that collects nuts
4. Up to 14 pounds

Answers on pg. 179

FIG WASP

She may be tiny, but the fig wasp plays a big part in keeping an important tree species alive—the fig tree! Thanks to her small size, she's able to enter a tiny hole and visit flowers found inside an unripe fig. Inside, she will lay her eggs while also pollinating some of the flowers with the pollen she carried with her, thanks to her Creature Power of Super Pollinate! Later, when the eggs hatch, the female wasps eventually leave with pollen and follow the smell emitted by other fig trees, where they repeat the fertilization process!

Not only does the fig wasp keep these trees alive, she also helps countless other creatures that rely on the fig tree too. Pigeons, toucans and monkeys are just some of the animals that feed on its fruits, which wouldn't exist without the fig wasp!

WASP WORDS

Can you find these words relating to the fig wasp?

TREE
POLLINATE
POLLEN
EGGS
FLOWERS
TINY
FIG
HATCH
PIGEONS
TOUCANS
MONKEYS

```
T B P M J G T R E E
P O P I G E O N S G
O M U J C T E F J F
L I O C F K G L B N
L H M N A P G O N F
I A L G K N S W H I
N T D J R E S E T G
A C I O E S Y R I P
T H E Z I V M S N K
E P O L L E N N Y U
```

Answers on pg. 179

FRUIT FLY

Time flies when you're learning about this guy! The fruit fly's life begins when he emerges from an egg as a larva. During this stage, the insect is a white, worm-shaped burrower that doesn't look anything like the flies you've probably seen hanging around your kitchen. He then enters the pupa stage, at which point he uses his Creature Power of Wing It On to begin developing his wings, six jointed legs and the bristly hairs on his body!

SHADOW MATCHING

Can you find the shadow that belongs to the fruit fly?

Answer on pg. 179

Fruit flies are attracted to ripened fruits and vegetables, but they're very adaptable and can lay eggs on many structures. This is one reason they are so resilient. They have been known to breed in drains, garbage disposals, empty bottles and cans, trash containers, mops and cleaning rags!

PURPLE MARTIN

Grab your passport, because this creature flies all the way to different countries! To escape the cold, the purple martin can migrate from North America to South American countries such as Brazil, sometimes traveling 13,700 miles in a year! When he gets thirsty along the way, he uses his Creature Power of Grab and Go to swoop down and scoop up water by skimming the surfaces of ponds and streams with his lower bill!

Ha, the meeting of the Martins! By migrating to warmer regions, the purple martin also enjoys longer days due to summer sunlight, which gives him extra time to hunt and feed during the nesting season.

Nice name, buddy!

ALL MIXED UP

Can you unscramble these words relating to the purple martin?

Answers on pg. 179

GMERTAI _____

LFY _____

ZBILRA _____

ILBL _____

NNETSGI _____

OSPWO _____

CSOPO _____

LUNA MOTH

The luna moth has one main purpose: to make more moths! Starting out as just a little egg then transforming into a colorful caterpillar, this cool creature eventually spins a cocoon and emerges as a moth when the timing is right. Once his wings expand and dry, the insect flies away in search of a mate to start the next generation. Thanks to his Creature Power of Snack Storage, he doesn't even have to eat on this journey! Instead, the luna moth simply survives on fat stored from the food he ate as a caterpillar.

If a luna moth still in his caterpillar stage feels threatened by predators, he can keep all kinds of creatures away by releasing a foul fluid from his mouth!

SPOT THE DIFFERENCE

Can you find the five differences between these two images of the luna moth?

Answers on pg. 179

CARIBBEAN FLAMINGO

This bright bird sure is unique! The Caribbean flamingo's beak bends downward, which helps with her unusual upside-down feeding lifestyle! To drink, she uses her Creature Power of Tongue Pump to rapidly pull in water with her long tongue, which can move in and out of her beak 6 times per second!

This bird must be quite the talker with a tongue like that!

That's true, bro! Before she even hatches, the Caribbean flamingo actually starts vocalizing while still in the egg! This form of communication helps with imprinting, which is a process that creates a bond between parents and babies and helps the bird announce she's coming out soon!

BIRDS OF A FEATHER

Can you match the Caribbean flamingo to her correct set of feathers?

Answer on pg. 179

DRAGONFISH

You can call this guy the master of bioluminescence, because he uses it for everything! All along his body, the dragonfish has photophores that create beams of light to communicate with other dragonfish. The dragonfish also uses bioluminescence for his Creature Power of Spy Vision! Under his eye, there's a red "spy light" that helps him see—but it can't be seen by other fish!

The light on the tip of the dragonfish's barbel can be used to confuse predators, and he can use it to attract his own prey!

What a handy tool to have attached to your head!

LIGHT THE WAY

Use bioluminescence to help the dragonfish find his way through this dark part of the ocean!

END

Answer on pg. 180

GIANT PACIFIC OCTOPUS

Defense is no problem for this smart aquatic creature! With her strong arms and ability to propel herself by shooting streams of water from her body like a jet, the giant Pacific octopus can make a quick escape from predators such as seals and sperm whales. Or, she can use her Creature Power of Cloudy Confusion to release an inky substance that makes it difficult for predators to see her swimming away!

The giant Pacific octopus can even change colors to avoid attacks! The pigments in her skin can change to match her surroundings—even if it's something complex in appearance like a coral reef!

HIDING SPOTS

Can you find the five giant Pacific octopuses
hiding in this image?

Answers on pg. 180

ELECTRIC EEL

The truth about this underwater animal might shock you! With thousands of electricity-producing cells in its body, the eel can create charges of 600 volts or more—that's more powerful than the wall sockets in your house! With his Creature Power of Shock Wave, this guy can use that electricity to stun his prey, which includes fish, frogs, reptiles and small mammals!

Wow, this guy is one shockingly powerful creature!

I sure wouldn't pick a fight with something as powerful as an electrical socket, but the electric eel does have to look out for larger predators! Fortunately, he can fend them off with a shock wave the same way he would stun his own prey!

JOLTED JUMBLE

The electric eel's Shock Wave has jumbled up these words! Can you unscramble each to reveal words relating to this creature's abilities, environment and diet?

DUWEERNRTA _____

CTELYCIIRTE _____

LSCEL _____

TNSU _____

SFHI _____

GROFS _____

OKHSC VEAW _____

Answers on pg. 180

BEAVER

This big rodent is strong, skilled and smart! To gather materials for his lodge, the beaver will first gnaw down a tree trunk. After the tree falls, he can use his Creature Power of Titan Teeth to pull the very heavy, long logs through the water! To carry smaller building materials such as sticks and twigs, he can use his hand-like paws!

The beaver is also a great communicator—especially when there's danger nearby. If he needs to warn his family of an approaching predator, this guy uses his tail like an alarm system by slapping it against the water to create a sound that can be heard from far away! This lets the other beavers know to jump in the water and retreat.

SWIM TO SAFETY

Can you help the beaver get through
the water and reach his lodge?

Answer on pg. 180

SOCKEYE SALMON

This fish encounters plenty of problems, but he always has a smart solution! Whether he needs to clear an obstacle, escape a predator or shake some sea lice loose, the sockeye salmon always has a good reason for jumping out of the water. Acting as a propeller, his tail (called a caudal fin) helps push him toward the surface. Then, using his Creature Power of Body Bend, the sockeye salmon contorts himself into an S- or C-shape in order to shoot himself up and forward!

He may be small, but this guy can reach some very impressive heights. The average sockeye salmon can clear a 6-to-7-foot waterfall!

This fish proves any-fin is possible!

FISHIN' FOR WORDS

Can you find these words relating to the sockeye salmon?

OBSTACLE
PROPELLER
WATERFALL
JUMPING
TAIL
SEA LICE
FIN
CONTORT
HEIGHTS
SMALL

Answers on pg. 180

```
P N S E A L I C E L
J R R R Z Q C S C Q
U G O H W O C O O O
M W F P Q A D T N B
P K I F E D Y A T S
I L N S T L L I O T
N S M A L L L L R A
G J U E J Z F E T C
H E I G H T S P R L
W A T E R F A L L E
```

BOWHEAD WHALE

This mammoth marine mammal gets her nutrients in amazing ways! Inside the bowhead whale's mouth are 640 baleen plates, which help her filter out huge volumes of ocean water when she grabs a mouthful of food. When it comes time to find the crustaceans, small fish and shrimp-like krill she likes to munch on, the bowhead whale uses her Creature Power of Sound Search to create echoes in the water that can pinpoint prey!

When the bowhead whale's echo bounces back to her, she knows it struck something in the area. This is called echolocation, and she also uses it to identify other whales and navigate through ice and tricky obstacles that might lie ahead!

So smart!

FOLLOW THE SOUND

Help the bowhead whale use her Creature Power of Sound Search to navigate obstacles and get to her food!

Answer on pg. 180

SEA OTTER

This agile creature has many traits and abilities that allow her to be an excellent swimmer. Thanks to her Creature Power of Propeller Tail, the sea otter can keep a strong forward momentum in the water! Once she gets going, she can use her webbed paws like flippers, and her legs, feet and tail to steer. Plus, her waterproof fur helps keep her skin dry!

Wow, she sure is built for the water!

Yeah, bro! The sea otter can also float on her back effortlessly. In fact, she's able to sleep, eat and groom all while floating on her back!

OTTER SPOTTING

Can you find the five differences between these sea otters?

Answers on pg. 181

GREAT WHITE SHARK

There's always a massive meal on the menu for this creature! Whales, dolphins, seabirds, seals and all sorts of fish are among the great white shark's favorite foods, and he's able to tear through them all very quickly. Thanks to his Creature Power of Fresh Teeth, he can grow new, super sharp teeth to replace any that are damaged and worn out!

The great white shark will sometimes eat especially large amounts of food at once, which can sustain him over a long period of time. When finding a big meal, like a seal, after going a while without eating, the shark may gorge on its prey and consume 10 to 20 percent of his body weight!

Holy mackerel—I mean, shark!

DEEP-SEA SEARCH

Can you find these words relating to the great white shark?

DOLPHINS   TEAR

WHALES   TEETH

SEALS   MASSIVE

SEABIRDS   BIG MEAL

FISH   PREY

```
H S B P H F R A Y G
M R E P R E Y G P D
A R X A C H X H Q O
S A S A B H E P S L
S W T B F I L P E P
I H E L Q I R W A H
V A A X U I S D L I
E L R Y Z I N H S N
E E J T E E T H F S
G S B I G M E A L B
```

Answers on pg. 181

BULL SHARK

This shark is quite the traveler, and that's no bull-oney! Because baby bull sharks are at risk from predators, a female bull shark will swim great distances from the ocean to estuaries or the mouths of rivers to give birth. Using her Creature Power of Motherly Instinct, she sometimes travels about 2,485 miles round trip, enduring environmental challenges that would harm or kill other marine animals!

Amazing!

It sure is! The bull shark will typically give birth to a litter of between one and 13 pups in the river mouth, and the young can stay there for about five years before venturing back into the ocean.

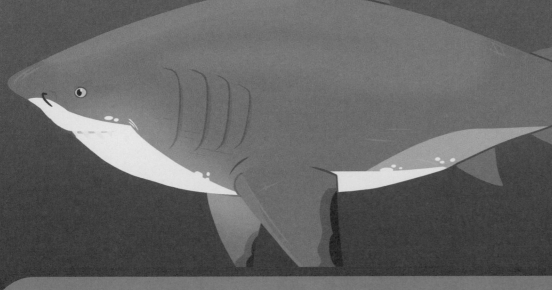

ALL JUM-BULLED UP

Can you unscramble the letters to reveal words relating to the bull shark?

DOTERPAR _____

WMSI _____

ANCEO _____

UPPS _____

SSNATIEDC _____

UTESSRAIE _____

VIRRSE _____

Answers on pg. 181

PLATYPUS

This unique creature has a bill similar to a duck's and webbed toes like a beaver's! But one of the platypus's most useful features is his tail. Thanks to his Creature Power of Multi-Tool Tail, he can propel and steer himself while swimming and even fold his dexterous tail to carry various items in the water and on land!

UNDERWATER MAZE

Help the platypus use his tail to steer through the water!

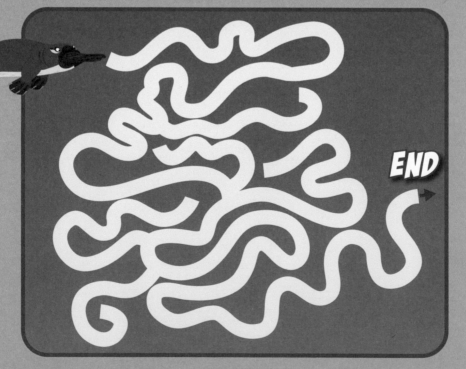

END

Answer on pg. 181

SEA URCHIN

It's easy to see how this guy got the nickname "porcupine of the sea"! The sea urchin's main protection against predators such as sea otters and eels is his hard, spiny shell, but he has other options. If an attacker tries to take a bite, the sea urchin's Creature Power of Toxic Taste releases a foul and harmful chemical in the predator's mouth!

SEA SCRAMBLE

Rearrange these letters to reveal words relating to the sea urchin!

YIPNS _____

LEHLS _____

ESA TORTES _____

LSEE _____

SLUSMES _____

LEKP _____

LHICAMEC _____

Answers on pg. 181

The sea urchin often chooses to look for his own food at night or deep in underwater crevices to avoid being found by predators. Plants and animals and everything in between are on the menu for this guy, including algae, mussels, kelp and even decaying matter, like dead fish.

BLUE MARLIN

Don't be blue—fun facts about a cool aquatic creature are here! Using his Creature Power of Migration Mission, the blue marlin follows warm waters and the prey found in them to travel great distances between feeding and reproduction areas. According to a study, one blue marlin was first observed in the western Atlantic Ocean and later seen in the Indian Ocean— an estimated distance of 9,254 miles!

That just "blue" my mind!

Ha! The blue marlin mostly lives in the epipelagic zone of the ocean, which ranges from the surface down to about 650 feet deep. Other creatures in this zone include dolphins, jellyfish and most sharks!

FISHIN' FOR WORDS

Can you find these words relating to the blue marlin?

AQUATIC   WATER   FEEDING
ATLANTIC   DISTANCE   DOLPHINS
OCEAN   SHARKS   JELLYFISH
MIGRATION

```
L J L S O P Q S Z D
F H E H H C E L X I
E T B L N A E P U S
E A J C L G R A F T
D Q O E A Y I K N A
I U B M O J F B S N
N A T L A N T I C C
G T A W A T E R S E
M I G R A T I O N H
I C D O L P H I N S
```

Answers on pg. 181

KRILL

This creature's daily life has a lot of ups and downs! The krill's feeding habits inform the use of his Creature Power of Aquatic Elevator—at night, he migrates toward the surface to graze on small organisms. During the day, he returns to deeper layers to avoid predators, digest food and rest!

When digesting, krill can descend 140 feet or more. Believe it or not, I can relate! Sometimes after eating a big meal, I like to sink deep into the couch!

KRILL IN THE BLANKS

Use the word bank to complete these sentences about the krill!

SURFACE   PREDATORS   DESCENDS

GRAZE   140 FEET   DIGESTING

FEEDING HABITS   MIGRATES

THE KRILL _____ _____ OR MORE WHEN

1   2

_____ . AT NIGHT, THE KRILL _____

3   4

TO THE _____ TO _____ .

5   6

THE KRILL'S _____ INFORM HIS

7

CREATURE POWER. THE KRILL RETURNS TO

DEEPER LAYERS TO AVOID _____ .

8

Answers on pg. 181

FLOUNDER

This flatfish has a life cycle unlike most fish under the sea! When she is young, the flounder's eyes are on the sides of her head and she swims in an upright position. Eventually, one of the eyes will move to the other side of her head and she will begin swimming sideways! Once she's a fully-formed adult, she gains the Creature Power of Body Bury, which allows her to escape predators by moving her fins up and down and burying herself in sand on the ocean floor!

FLOUNDER FINDER

Can you find five flounders hiding in their habitat?

When the flounder is young, her diet consists of worms called polychaetes, small fish and crustaceans. As an adult, she becomes more of an opportunistic eater as she eats the likes of anchovies, pinfish, pigfish, shrimp, mollusks and other invertebrates. I totally get it! One of the best parts of growing up is finding new foods you enjoy eating!

Answers on pg. 182

BRINE SHRIMP

You're not looking at this page the wrong way—this shrimp typically swims upside down! On his thorax, the brine shrimp has 11 pairs of feather-like legs, and he actually breathes through his feet! The brine shrimp's legs are also crucial to his swimming strategy: Using his Creature Power of Underwater Drumming, he beats his legs rhythmically to propel himself through the water!

TRUE OR FALSE

Use your knowledge of the brine shrimp to decide if each statement is true or false!

_____ **1.** The brine shrimp swims upside down.

_____ **2.** The brine shrimp has a total of 11 legs.

_____ **3.** The brine shrimp breathes through his feather-like nostrils.

_____ **4.** The sun affects the way the brine shrimp swims.

_____ **5.** The brine shrimp swims by propelling himself with his strong tail fin.

The brine shrimp is naturally attracted to light sources, which is one reason he's often found swimming upside down when the sun is overhead. I can relate—I like to hang out on my back under the sun, too!

Answers on pg. 182

DOG-FACED WATER SNAKE

This snake sure knows the meaning of growing up! Unlike some other reptile species that lay eggs, the dog-faced water snake gives birth to baby snakes, which are sometimes only about 6 inches in length. As they mature, though, they can grow to be up to 3.3 feet long! And to help that happen, this reptile uses the Creature Power of Snack Attack to swallow prey whole!

SPOT THE DIFFERENCE

Circle the five differences between these images of the dog-faced water snake!

Answers on pg. 182

The dog-faced water snake is most often found in salt and brackish waters, but she occasionally lives in freshwater environments, too. She is an important part of her habitat—her strong appetite actually helps keep certain fish populations from growing out of control!

GIANT MANTA RAY

Τhis fish is the largest type of ray in the world! The giant manta ray's body is covered in scales called dermal denticles, which can help reduce turbulence and allow him to swim more efficiently. Once he picks up speed, the giant manta ray can even eject himself to the surface of the water and use his Creature Power of Wide Glide to stretch his 29-foot wingspan and glide atop the water's surface!

MANTA MAZE

Help the giant manta ray swim to the surface of the water!

Answer on pg. 182

RED SNAPPER

This big fish can measure 40 inches in length and weigh 50 pounds or more! The red snapper gets his intimidating name from his enlarged canine teeth, which help him chow down on a variety of prey. With his Creature Power of Snap Action, he bites into the likes of plankton, worms, crab, shrimp, octopus and squid!

SNAPPER SEARCH

Can you find these words relating to the red snapper?

CANINE
TEETH
PLANKTON
WORMS
OCTOPUS
SNAP ACTION
CHOW DOWN
SQUID
CRAB
SHRIMP

```
S T L Z F J I J E J
W N P L A N K T O N
W S A O C E P E L C
O Z H P C D N E E A
R S Q R A T R T Y N
M X Q H I C O H U I
S C S U J M T P F N
D R W E I J P I U E
S A Z K Z D T M O S
Z B C H O W D O W N
```

Answers on pg. 182

Gather round for the tale of the tail of the humpback whale! This massive mammal's tail fin is called a fluke, and it can reach widths of 18 feet! She uses her fluke for her Creature Power of Super Propellor, which allows her to zoom through the water at speeds between 8 and 11 miles per hour and even breach the surface if she needs to communicate with other whales!

The humpback whale's fluke is serrated (kind of like a bread knife!) and pointed at the tips. The color patterns, size and shape can be quite different from whale to whale, which is why the fluke can be used to identify a humpback—like fingerprints with humans!

SPOT THE DIFFERENCE

Can you find the five differences between these two images of the humpback whale?

Answers on pg. 182

PACIFIC WALRUS

Time to get s-pacific about the walrus! In spring, the Pacific walrus and her young migrate north to follow the edge of the sea ice. When it's time to eat along the journey, her Creature Power of Whisker Fishing allows her to use her hundreds of highly sensitive whiskers to sense prey, such as clams, as she searches the seafloor! She can consume about 50 to 60 clams in one dive!

The Pacific walrus's dives are epic journeys themselves! She can go to depths beyond 328 feet and remain submerged for over 20 minutes!

I'm deeply impressed!

TUSK TASK

Find the walruses with missing tusks, then draw them in! Once you're done, tally up the tusks you added!

_____ TUSKS

Answers on pg. 183

LOGGERHEAD SEA TURTLE

This sea-going reptile spends the majority of her life in the big, blue ocean! With her Creature Power of Going the Distance, she can swim many, many miles to find feeding grounds or a sandy beach, where she can deposit her eggs to start a new generation of little loggerheads!

SEA SEARCH

Can you find these words relating to the loggerhead sea turtle?

REPTILE
SWIM
EGGS
SAND
FLEEING
OCEAN
DISTANCE
FEEDING
BEACH
GENERATION

Answers on pg. 183

```
F M K E V G S W I M
E D W E I E R G R Q
E Q I Q Q N Q E E I
D O F S H E D G P B
I C L R T R U G T E
N E E S Z A I S I A
G A E A I T N C L C
T N I N J I F C E H
V Y N D U O U S E J
T E G J P N E T P W
```

SALMON SHARK

While most fish are cold-blooded, the salmon shark gets the best of both worlds by having both cold and warm blood vessels! His cold blood vessels are laid out next to the warm ones, which helps heat up the flowing blood! With his Creature Power of Perfect Temp, this guy can maintain a body temperature of about 60 degrees F above the surrounding water temperature!

The salmon shark gets his name from his favorite food, the Pacific salmon. But he's not a picky eater! This large shark also chows down on sablefish, squid, herring and a variety of other fish it finds in the Pacific Ocean.

I'm glad I'm not named after my favorite food! Though "Chocolate Cake Kratt" does have a nice ring to it....

SNACK SEEKER

Can you help the salmon shark find five salmon hidden in this underwater habitat?

Answers on pg. 183

ORANGUTAN

This ape is great at making use of his resources! The orangutan uses stones and twigs to obtain and process food, large leaves to create shelter from rain and he even uses tree branches as fly swatters! Plus, thanks to his Creature Power of Mental Map, this guy is able to remember specific details about his surroundings, such as the locations of trees that carry the fruits he eats!

The orangutan is only found in two places on Earth: the islands of Borneo and Sumatra. Currently, there are three species of orangutan, and one of them, the Tapanuli orangutan, is the rarest great ape species in the world!

APE MAZE

Help the orangutan use his Creature Power of Mental Map to find his way to the fruit tree!

END

Answer on pg. 183

LEAFCUTTER ANT

This insect knows the meaning of teamwork! The leafcutter ant works together with her fellow ants to bring pieces of leaves, stems and petals back to her nest, which then grow into the fungus she feeds on. Using her Creature Power of Leaf Lift, she can carry vegetation eight times heavier than her own body weight!

Once she cuts a piece of leaf to carry in her mandible, the smaller ant on the team hitches a ride on the leaf. That leafcutter ant's role is to watch the worker's back for phorid flies that may try to land on the ant and deposit their eggs!

Wow, it pays to have a friend to watch your back!

LIFT OR LEAVE?

Use the leafcutter ant's ability to lift vegetation eight times her body weight to determine whether she should lift these leaves or leave them alone!

4 MG

48 MG
☐ LIFT
☐ LEAVE

26 MG
☐ LIFT
☐ LEAVE

28 MG
☐ LIFT
☐ LEAVE

30 MG
☐ LIFT
☐ LEAVE

36 MG
☐ LIFT
☐ LEAVE

31 MG
☐ LIFT
☐ LEAVE

Answers on pg. 183

AFRICAN WILDCAT

When it comes to hunting, this cat doesn't let anything stand in her way! The incredibly athletic African wildcat can chase after her prey at speeds exceeding 30 miles per hour! And if she encounters an obstacle, she can use her Creature Power of Ultra Jump to leap about 6 feet in the air! Best of all, she doesn't always need the running start to perform this impressive feat!

WILDCAT WORDS

Can you find these words relating to the African wildcat?

JUMP   ATHLETIC

HUNTING   LEAP

PREY   RUNNING

AFRICA   BIRDS

OBSTACLE   HARES

Answers on pg. 183

```
A O A H D U V Q H L
T Y B X U B D Z A E
H J J S W N B B R A
L A U P T S T U E P
E F M R Z A Z I S G
T R P E Y F C U N C
I I G Y Z R Z L I G
C C H H X M R G E G
L A I R U N N I N G
Z B I R D S J K K Y
```

Mice, medium-size birds, hares and some lizards are all on the menu for the African wildcat. She is such a skilled hunter, she can even catch her prey in midair!

GRAY WOLF

This communicative creature is capable of many calls including barks, snarls and growls, but she's best known for her Creature Power of Signature Howl! This ability allows the gray wolf to be heard from about 6 miles away depending on her environment, and she uses it for everything from expressing her mood to identifying members of her pack!

Each member of a gray wolf pack has her own unique howl. When the whole pack howls together in a chorus, the sound can last anywhere from 30 seconds to two minutes! It might not be music to your ears, but it sure is amazing!

SCRAMBLED SOUNDS

Unscramble these words relating to the gray wolf, then use the letters in the boxes to write out her Signature Howl!

FOLW ___ ___ ☐ ___ ___ ___

CAOVL ___ ☐ ___ ___ ___ ___

DOMO ___ ☐ ☐ ___

WROLG ___ ___ ☐ ___ ☐ ___

SIGNATURE HOWL: H _ _ _ _ _ _ _ _ _ L!

Answers on pg. 184

97

LION

This big cat sure makes his voice heard! Thanks to his Creature Power of Extraordinary Roar, the lion can let out a mighty roar to reach separated members of his social group, which is called a pride, up to 5 miles away! Plus, he can use it to keep other creatures away from his territory!

Not only can the lion make himself heard from far away, he can also hear other creatures from quite a distance. By rotating his ears side to side, he can hear sounds made by potential prey about 1 mile away!

If I said I wasn't impressed, I'd be "lion!"

MANE EVENT

Can you help this lion find his way through the maze to the other members of his pride?

Answer on pg. 184

FOSSA

This cat-like mammal has some serious tree-climbing skills! The fossa has semi-retractable claws and flexible ankles that allow her to climb up and down trees headfirst and a 26-inch tail that she uses to hug the bark behind her when traveling for that extra stability! With her Creature Power of Balancing Act, the fossa uses her tail for balance as she leaps from branch to branch pursuing prey such as lemurs!

The fossa is a top predator in Madagascar, which is the only place she can be found! When she's not hunting the likes of lemurs in trees, she goes after insects, lizards, birds, fish and small mammals including pigs and mice.

FOSSA WORD FINDER

Can you find these words relating to the fossa?

TREES   CLAWS
TAIL   CLIMBING
MAMMAL   ANKLES
BALANCE   PREY
PREDATOR   LEMURS

Answers on pg. 184

```
F A M B A N K L E S
N L C A R Z A Z G V
N E P L M U L P S C
N M R A I M C S O L
F U E N O M A K Z A
P R D C C T B L S W
R S A E J Q A I N S
E E T H E Q J I N J
Y R O T Y D X D L G
U U R A J T R E E S
```

HONEY BADGER

This guy is known for his aggression, and he's got the intense sounds to back it up! With his Creature Power of Deafening Defense, he can keep potential predators such as hyenas away by releasing a loud snarl or a guttural growl! But young honey badgers are a different story: When they're in distress, they make little hiccup sounds!

The honey badger can have a very large range that he considers home, and he uses scent marks to communicate his territory to other badgers. Humans leave scent markings around their homes too—when they forget to pick up dirty laundry!

MAKING A MARK

Help the honey badger make his way through this territory to leave his scent markings!

END

Answer on pg. 184

DOMESTIC PIG

Say hello to one of the hungriest mammals on the farm! The domestic pig's diet is pretty well-rounded, consisting of plenty of protein, grains, grasses, vegetables, hay, corn, nuts and meat scraps. And if she ever finds herself out in the wild in need of food, she can use her Creature Power of Super Snout to smell something as far as 25 feet underground!

Nice nose! What's also amazing about the domestic pig is how quickly she can grow. A growing young piglet can double her weight in just one week! And an adult domestic pig can weigh anywhere from 110 to 770 pounds!

SPOT THE DIFFERENCE

Can you find the five differences between these two images of the domestic pig?

Answers on pg. 184

Take it from us—the "wild" part of this dog's name is no joke! The African wild dog can roam in packs ranging from six to 20, which means it's easy for the group not to notice right away when a member gets separated. If that happens, she can use her Creature Power of Hoot and Holler to let out an owl-like "hoo" call that the missing members can hear from 2 to 3 miles away!

While this dog is impressive, the lion still reigns supreme in Africa. However, when a large pack of African wild dogs work together, they can sometimes manage to steal freshly killed prey from a few lions! Pretty bold if you ask me!

Now that's a grab-and-go meal!

WILD WORDS

Can you find these words relating to the African wild dog?

PACK   GROUP
HOOT   MEMBERS
HOLLER   PREY
CALL   LIONS
ROAM   STEAL

```
Y L G R O U P W R L
A I O M R O A M Q Z
E O C C E K D B Q R
S N X H A M L F R T
B S K A O L B N Q F
G P S H S L L E L U
P Y T O K P L M R F
R X E O D J A E M S
E S A T S G W C R P
Y O L O D E Q E K B
```

Answers on pg. 185

DWARF GECKO

This little guy is one agile reptile! The dwarf gecko's hands and feet are covered in very tiny hair-like projections known as setae, and each seta has even more structures that have flattened ends called spatulae. Thanks to the gecko's Creature Power of Super Stick, the surfaces of his hands and feet create electrostatic forces that allow him to stick to almost anything!

Talk about sticking the landing!

WHERE'D THE GECKO GO?

Can you find five dwarf geckos sticking to the surfaces in this image?

Answers on pg. 185

This reptile's tail also comes into play when he's making a climb. The dwarf gecko uses his tail for balance and stability when he scurries across narrow branches and leaves.

AFRICAN ELEPHANT

This amazing mammal makes one of the lowest frequency sounds of any creature studied by scientists so far—in fact, some of the African elephant's calls can't even be heard by human ears! Thanks to her Creature Power of Ready to Rumble, her low rumbling sound can be heard by other elephants about 6 miles away! She can use it to attract a mate or to let other herds know her herd is nearby so they don't compete for food.

The African elephant is very smart, which means she knows how to be strategic with her sounds. Often, she'll emit her rumbling sounds at dawn or dusk when there's less noise pollution in the air, meaning other animals aren't filling the area with their own competing sounds!

RUMBLE JUMBLE

Can you unscramble these words relating
to the African elephant?

LMMMAA _____

BLUMRING _____

RHDE _____

REQFUEYCN _____

NSSDUO _____

WDNA _____

USDK _____

Answers on pg. 185

BENGAL TIGER

This big cat has a big appetite to match! Being one of the top predators in Asia, there's not much the Bengal tiger can't catch for dinner. Using her Creature Power of Clever Camouflage, she can blend into the jungle background before ambushing her prey, which includes birds, reptiles and even young elephants and rhinos!

HOWLER MONKEY

Listen up—this is one of the loudest creatures on Earth! Living in trees with social groups ranging from five to 18 fellow howler monkeys, this mammal is known for the incredible volume he's able to produce thanks to an enlarged bone in his throat. Using his Creature Power of Rowdy Roar, he can make his voice heard from up to 3 miles away!

The howler monkey's Rowdy Roar has a variety of purposes. He can use it to defend food resources, mark his territory or even attract a mate.

Sorry bro, what? I didn't hear a word you said!

MONKEY JUMBLE

Can you unscramble these words relating to the howler monkey?

SERET _____

HOATTR _____

MECSAR _____

DUSTLEO _____

CVEIO _____

MULEVO _____

DWORY RRAO _____

Answers on pg. 185

EUROPEAN HEDGEHOG

With a body covered in about 5,000 sharp spines, this is one tough little mammal! When he needs to defend himself from predators such as foxes or badgers, the European hedgehog uses his Creature Power of Spiky Shield to curl up into a ball and stick his spines straight up!

HIDING HEDGEHOGS

Can you find the five European hedgehogs hiding in their habitat?

Looking sharp, buddy! A baby hedgehog is born with more than 150 sharp spines, but in order to protect the mother, the spines are covered by a fluid-filled membrane. After about a day, the covering dries and falls off. As he gets older, he continues to grow many more spines!

Answers on pg. 185

SAMBAR DEER

This herbivorous mammal loves to eat leaves, grasses, fruits, stems, berries and bark, but he always has to be sure he's not about to be eaten himself! With his keen senses of smell and sight, the sambar deer can detect nearby predators such as Bengal tigers, leopards and crocodiles. If he senses a threat, he uses his Creature Power of Honk Alarm to make a loud sound that warns his fellow deer and other creatures they may be in danger!

SPOT THE DEER-FERENCE

Can you find the five differences between these two sambar deer?

While he spends most of his time on land, the sambar deer is a great swimmer! This skill comes in handy when he needs to escape a predator that can't swim!

OSTRICH

Meet the fastest-running bird in the world! With her powerful, long legs, the ostrich uses her Creature Power of Lightning Limbs to reach speeds of 40 miles per hour as she escapes predators such as cheetahs, lions and leopards! And while she may not fly, the ostrich does use her wings to help her turn while running (similar to the rudders of a ship) or to shade her baby chicks!

Not only is she the fastest, the ostrich also lays the biggest eggs of any bird! Multiple ostriches will typically lay their eggs together in a routine known as clutch dumping. Once they arrive, some eggs can be about the size of a grapefruit!

Now that's a fruitful bird!

BIRD WORD FINDER

Can you find and circle these words relating to the ostrich?

LEGS	WINGS
EGGS	ESCAPE
FASTEST	RUNNING

```
F S G N I W U U T
A E Y V A K U H R
S K P X E G G S U
T H Z A N O S S N
E B Z Z C P K E N
S Z G S M S I W I
T Q G E W W E U N
W E C U Q P D P G
L I D H W R X Q O
```

Answers on pg. 186

119

INDIAN LEOPARD

Look up in the trees, it's an Indian leopard! When she's not sleeping in trees during the day to stay away from predators such as lions, this big cat likes to hunt anything from large birds to reptiles to deer. Using her Creature Power of Capture and Carry, the Indian leopard will sometimes bring prey up to 1½ times her own body weight up into a tree to keep it away from a fellow predator!

When it comes to hunting, the Indian leopard is super sneaky! Her spots act as a camouflage that allows her to remain hidden. Since her prey doesn't see her coming, it doesn't have the chance to escape!

SPOT THE DIFFERENCE

Find the five differences between these two images of the Indian leopard!

Answers on pg. 186

EGYPTIAN COBRA

This snake is one of the largest cobras found in all of Africa! The Egyptian cobra's scales help him with everything from retaining moisture inside his body to just getting around. The scales on the bottom of his body can be used to grip the ground and create friction, which, along with muscles, pushes him forward. While fleeing the scene is his preferred method for dealing with predators, this guy can use his Creature Power of Venom Defense to strike an attacker with his sharp, venomous fangs!

Not only does he fight off predators, the Egyptian cobra is a predator himself! This carnivorous reptile feeds on various birds, mammals, lizards, insects and even other snakes!

COBRA CROSSWORD

Use the clues below to complete this crossword
about the Egyptian cobra!

ACROSS

3. The Egyptian cobra's method for defense
   before resorting to venom
5. Animal group with fur or hair eaten by the
   Egyptian cobra
8. Useful feature covering the cobra's body
9. Prey that is the cobra's own kind

DOWN

1. The cobra's venomous teeth
2. Attacker of prey
4. Animal group consisting
   of bugs eaten by the
   Egyptian cobra
6. Continent in which
   the Egyptian
   cobra lives
7. Feathered animals
   eaten by the
   Egyptian cobra

Answers on pg. 186

KOALA

Cute, cuddly and equipped to climb, the koala is one incredible creature! This guy spends his days sleeping, eating, grooming and foraging in the trees of Australia, and he's great at getting up there. The rough skin on the pads of his paws provides good grip against trees, and he also has two thumbs on each forepaw to help him climb. When he needs a very tight grip around branches, the koala uses his **Creature Power of Claw Hook** to secure himself!

While he is an excellent climber, the koala actually moves a little quicker on the ground. Running like a rabbit, he can reach speeds between 4 and 6 miles per hour. I can eat between four and six slices of pizza per hour, but I never run after a meal like that!

KOALA TERMS

Can you find these words relating to the koala?

AUSTRALIA   FORAGING   PAWS

CLIMB   SLEEPING   THUMB

BRANCHES   EATING   GROOMING

CLAW HOOK

```
A C G R O O M I N G
I U L K R B T O Z F
T B S A V P S Z C O
H E R T W F W L L R
U A X A R H S D I A
M T E P N A O B M G
B I K A X C L O B I
P N R W Z M H I K N
C G W S A P E E A G
S L E E P I N G S I
```

Answers on pg. 186

GIANT PANDA

Now here's a creature with a favorite food—the giant panda can eat between 20 and 40 pounds of bamboo a day! With his large head and strong bite force, this guy uses his Creature Power of Muscle Mouth to chew through all the toughest parts of the plant, including the leaves, stems, shoots and thick outer sheath!

If you think the giant panda ever gets tired of munching on bamboo, guess again! About 12 to 14 hours of this mammal's day is spent either foraging for a feast or eating one. That's a real passion for food!

BAMBOOZLED!

Can you unscramble these words relating
to the giant panda?

OBOMAB _____

ALMAMM _____

VEELAS _____

EMSTS _____

TEBI RECFO _____

CLUSEM OHMTU _____

NLATP _____

Answers on pg. 187

GIRAFFE

As far as parenting goes, the giraffe stands head and shoulders above others! A mother usually gives birth to just one infant at a time, and that infant is sometimes already 6 feet tall! Thanks to her tall height and large eyes, the mother giraffe is great at detecting threats. If she needs to defend her young, she can use her Creature Power of Swift Strike to deliver front and rear kicks to the attacker!

Baby giraffes can stand up on their feet just 20 minutes after being born! About 10 hours later, they can already run!

Incredible!

TALL TERMS

Can you find these words relating to the giraffe?

MOTHER   EYES
YOUNG   KICKS
HEIGHT   STAND
TALL   DEFEND

```
W N L W F O J K U J
E S S T U O H I I S
Y O U N G O E C M T
O K N F H K I K O A
Z D E Y E S G S T N
Y W E T X E H C H D
S Y F F A V T B E G
H S V Q E L A X R R
O W I K N N L M R N
J W K J Q L D I T D
```

Answers on pg. 187

129

ERMINE

This creature truly changes with the seasons! Also known as a stoat or short-tailed weasel, the small ermine is prone to attacks from predators such as foxes, coyotes and goshawks. But thanks to her Creature Power of Cryptic Coloration, she can camouflage herself to blend in with both the white snow in winter and the brown branches, grasses, wooden stumps and fallen logs in the summer!

ERMINE MAZE

Can you help the ermine make her way through this snowy habitat?

Answer on pg. 187

END

The ermine's fur begins to change color based on changes in daylength and temperature. In the winter, she even gains additional dense fur on the soles of her feet to protect against the cold!

Stoat-ally awesome!

KOMODO DRAGON

Meet the biggest lizard in the world! The male Komodo dragon measures about 10 feet in total length—and his muscular tail can often account for half his length! He uses it for his Creature Power of Tail Whip: If prey such as small deer or pigs are within range, the Komodo dragon whips his tail with fierce might to take them down!

DRAGON JUMBLE

Can you unscramble these words relating to the Komodo dragon?

ZIRDLA _____

ETHET _____

ALTI HPWI _____

REDE _____

LWSCA _____

GPI _____

ERPY _____

CSUULRAM _____

Answers on pg. 187

Very handy hunting tools!

That's not all this guy can do to take down prey! The Komodo dragon also has long claws on his feet, sharp teeth and venomous toxins from glands in his jaw!

GREEN IGUANA

Look up in the trees if you want to see this guy! Using his Creature Power of Mighty Climb, the green iguana uses his claws to hook into a tree while his long tail helps him keep his balance on the way up! Once he finds a spot to settle on in the tree, he will bob his head to let others know that he owns that territory.

That's awesome!

And that's not all, bro—the green iguana is also a very capable swimmer! If he needs to traverse a body of water, he can use his back legs and his long, muscular tail to propel him forward!

CLIMB AND CLAIM

Help the green iguana use his Creature Power of Mighty Climb to make his way up this tree and claim his territory!

START

END

Answer on pg. 187

ANOLE LIZARD

This lizard may be little, but he eats just about anything he can fit in his mouth! Butterflies, moths, ants, beetles, spiders and mollusks are all on the menu for the anole lizard, and he uses his Creature Power of Awesome Ambush to suddenly leap onto his prey! That ability also comes in handy when this guy finds another creature foraging in his territory.

The anole lizard is cold-blooded, so if he's feeling a little too cold, he will spend some time basking in the sunlight. If he starts to feel too warm, he can regulate his body temperature by finding shady shelter. I can relate, little guy—comfort is key!

LOOK-ALIKE LIZARDS

Can you find the five differences between these anole lizards?

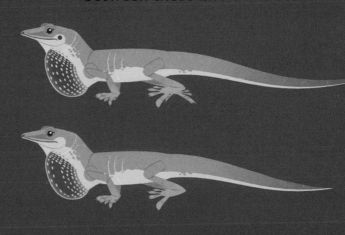

Answers on pg. 187

AARDVARK

This creature's features are built for finding her favorite foods underground! The aardvark's long snout contains specialized bones that enhance her sense of smell, which helps her locate little invertebrates such as termites and ants. When a nest is found, she uses her Creature Power of Shovel Claws to break through the mound's tough exterior, creating an entryway for her sticky tongue to reach the insects living inside! In just one night, she can consume roughly 50,000 insects!

Holy hunger!

The aardvark also uses her powerful claws and limbs to build complex burrows to use as shelter for her young or hiding places from predators. These burrows have been known to reach 43 feet in length and are often used by many other species seeking protection from extreme weather conditions!

CREATURE CROSSWORD

Use the clues to complete this crossword about the aardvark!

ACROSS

3. Shelter built by the aardvark
5. Wood-eating invertebrate eaten by the aardvark
6. Long feature containing specialized bones

DOWN

1. 50,000 can be eaten by the aardvark in one night
2. The aardvark's sharp feature used to make shelter
4. Sense used by the aardvark to find invertebrates
5. Sticky aardvark feature used to reach a meal of insects

Answers on pg. 188

RIVER OTTER

This cuddly creature can be found near the lakes, marshes, rivers and swamps of North America! And when winter comes, the river otter doesn't retreat—instead, she makes great use of the conditions! Using her Creature Power of Snow Dive, the river otter will slide down snowbanks and burrow through the snow, which is not only fun but helps her strengthen social bonds, practice hunting techniques and scent-mark her habitat!

That's snow smart!

ODD OTTER OUT

Can you find the river otter that doesn't look like the others?

Answer on pg. 188

Good one, bro! Since the river otter is always active, she works up quite an appetite. Throughout the day, she'll chow down on a variety of foods: amphibians, fish, turtles, crayfish, crabs, birds and their eggs, small mammals and aquatic plants!

PRAIRIE DOG

Meet the master of digging burrows! This rodent lives in a large colony with his fellow prairie dogs, and his extensive burrow systems—which feature two or more openings and separate rooms for nesting and nursing—are built away from obstructing rocks and plants so that he can see clearly in all directions. If he does detect an approaching predator, the prairie dog uses his Creature Power of Complex Communication to tell the other members of the colony details about the threat!

Like humans, the prairie dog's vocalizations include nouns, verbs and adjectives! This special way of speaking allows them to tell other family members specific information such as whether or not a predator is venomous, if a human is approaching or if a coyote is moving at high speeds nearby!

Wow, I want to learn how to speak prairie dog!

CREATURE QUIZ

Can you answer these questions about the prairie dog?

1. What parts of speech do prairie dogs use to communicate?
A. Nouns, adjectives, symbols
B. Nouns, verbs, adjectives
C. Melodies, verbs, gerunds

2. The prairie dog lives in a large group called a
A. Society
B. Flock
C. Colony

3. What are the separate rooms in this creature's burrow for?
A. Nesting and nursing
B. Reading and relaxing
C. Feasting and fasting

4. Which threat do prairie dogs communicate about?
A. Venomous predators
B. Fast coyotes
C. All of the above

Answers on pg. 188

LOWLAND STREAKED TENREC

This guy has plenty of options for defending himself! Covered in black and yellow detachable quills, the lowland streaked tenrec is equipped to ward off predators, such as large snakes and mongooses. He can also use his Creature Power of Hard Headbutt to scare away creatures that come too close!

TENREC TERMS

Can you find these words relating to the lowland streaked tenrec?

QUILLS
BLACK
YELLOW
TEETH
DIG
SNAKES
MONGOOSES
HEADBUTT

Answers on pg. 188

```
T U Q S R P X A T O
B O H U O P A P T B
S C B E I F Q Q T X
N K W L A L P S E Y
A I A D A D L H E T
K G W D I C B S T Y
E A K M D G K U H C
S W C R B Q Z I T T
M O N G O O S E S T
W V E J Y E L L O W
```

And that's not all this tough defender can do! The lowland streaked tenrec can bite or quickly run into his burrow to escape a threat. Plus, his unique color helps him blend into his surroundings!

143

CLAM

This creature doesn't need hands, fins or claws to be an expert digger! Using her Creature Power of Fleshy Foot, the clam extends her muscular appendage down into the sand or mud in the direction she wants to go. Then, she takes water into her siphon and releases it out the other end where the foot is anchored, which loosens up the sand around it and allows the shell to inch deeper!

The clam usually digs to get away from approaching predators, such as blue crabs, starfish or gulls. In just a matter of seconds, she can dig as deep as 1 to 2 feet! That's some serious strength!

CLAM SCRAMBLE

Can you unjumble these words relating to the clam?

ELHLS _____

OFTO _____

ADNS _____

NROCAH _____

EATRW _____

SABCR _____

RIFSHSAT _____

LULSG _____

Answers on pg. 188

BUSH DOG

Whether he needs shelter, protection for his young or just a place to rest, this canine has no trouble making himself at home in the burrows built by other creatures. And if the bush dog is hungry when he happens upon the burrow of a creature, such as an armadillo, he uses his Creature Power of Mighty Dig to quickly tear into the dirt and retrieve his prey! Then, he has a meal and a place to stay!

The bush dog has a unique feature not seen in most canines: webbed feet! These help him when he needs to swim, which he's also very good at!

That's pretty handy! Or should I say footy?

DIGGING FOR WORDS

Can you find these words relating
to the bush dog?

CANINE
WEBBED
ARMADILLO
DIG
PREY
DIRT
BURROWS
SWIM

Answers on pg. 189

```
Q B H K C A N I N E
T U X B E B S B V N
I S L E O B W U I E
P B T C W X I R W L
L R F J X Y M R L C
Q Y E I V F X O E N
D R D Y E J F W W D
I P G K Y K Y S Z I
G B W E B B E D F R
A R M A D I L L O T
```

VOLE

While others are hibernating for the winter, this cool creature is staying active underground! The vole lives in a subnivean zone, which is an open, shallow area found between layers of snow and terrain that can maintain a temperature around 32 degrees F—regardless of how cold it is above ground! She's also great at keeping her body well-insulated: Thanks to her Creature Power of Massive Meal, this little critter can eat 60 percent of her body weight in just 24 hours!

The vole is very crafty when it comes to making the subnivean zone feel like home. She creates elaborate pathways and different chambers, including a sleep site, a bathroom and an eating quarters where she stores foods such as seeds and tubers!

ODD ONE OUT

Can you find the vole that doesn't look like the others?

Answer on pg. 189

SAND CAT

Found in the Sahara Desert, the Arabian Peninsula and Central Asia, the sand cat knows how to keep his cool! His heavily furred feet help him walk on the hot surface of the sand, but he's also great at digging an underground escape from the sun! And when he needs to avoid predatory threats above ground, the sand cat can use his Creature Power of Crouching Camo to lower himself to the ground and perfectly blend in thanks to his body's coloration!

The sand cat can survive on little to no water, which comes in handy while living in the desert. Most of his water comes from his diet of birds, lizards, snakes, bugs and mammals, which he usually hunts for at night when temperatures are cooler.

ALL JUMBLED UP

Unscramble these words relating
to the sand cat!

TREESD_____

ACMO_____

EWTRA_____

NSAD_____

ETEF_____

DRSBI_____

ZIRDLAS_____

GBUS_____

Answers on pg. 189

American Alligator

heck out this mighty reptile! While the adult American alligator doesn't need to burrow to hide from predators like many other creatures do, he can dig holes for nesting or bury himself in mud during difficult weather. And when he's hungry, he situates himself beneath the surface of the water, sitting motionless sometimes for hours, waiting to use his Creature Power of Snack Attack to quickly chomp down on many types of fish, mammals, birds, rodents, hooved animals, reptiles and amphibians!

In colder seasons, the American alligator can sit still in partially frozen water with his snout sticking out above the surface until it melts! As he regulates his body temperature beneath the frozen layer, he can tolerate cold waters of about 35 to 39 degrees F!

So cool! Literally!

ALLIGATOR LOCATOR

Can you find five alligators hiding in this habitat?

Answers on pg. 189

PANGOLIN

This creature may not have great eyesight, but he doesn't need it to find his favorite foods! The pangolin has a great sense of smell and sensitive hearing, which helps him find ants and termites in mounds or in the ground by picking up the faintest sounds and vibrations! Once he finds a feast, he'll dig into the mound with his claws then use his Creature Power of Towering Tongue to snatch up the prey with his incredibly long, muscular tongue!

TONGUE-TASTIC TERMS

Can you find these words relating to the pangolin?

TERMITES   CLAWS

ANTS   SMELL

MOUNDS   HEARING

VIBRATIONS   TONGUE

Answers on pg. 189

```
L E E C L A W S T A
V M X M T O N G U E
L O Y D S N C S J H
H U U X A M M Y A M
U N V A F N E W Z X
V D E G C B T L Y R
B S T O L E C S L M
T E R M I T E S R Z
H E A R I N G Q J O
V I B R A T I O N S
```

In relation to his body size, the pangolin has one of the longest tongues in the animal kingdom! It can range from about 6 to 15 inches in length, and sometimes it's even longer than the pangolin's body itself!

Wow, I'd be getting tongue-tied all the time if I were him!

NORWAY LEMMING

T his guy may be small, but you don't want to mess with his burrow! The Norway lemming will either dig his own or settle into a preexisting burrow in mountainous, flat or even frozen arctic areas. Rather than hide when an intruder approaches his territory, the Norway lemming uses his Creature Power of Mighty Defender to lunge, bite and chase away threats!

When it comes to protecting his territory, the Norway lemming often takes on threats many times his size! He's been known to defend against cats, large birds and even humans!

SPOT THE DIFFERENCE

Can you find five differences between these two images of the Norway lemming?

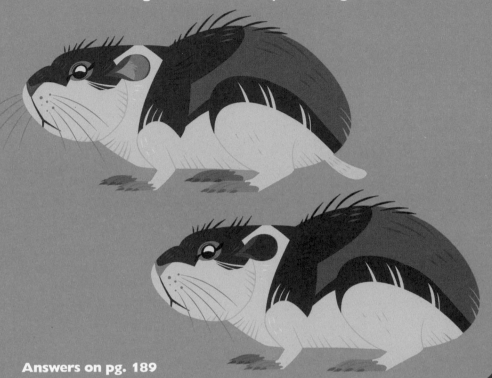

Answers on pg. 189

GOLIATH TARANTULA

This massive arachnid lives up to his name! Once the Goliath tarantula takes over the burrow of another creature (sometimes by overpowering and eating it!), he builds a trip wire made from his silk to alert him of nearby prey. When prey comes along, he uses his Creature Power of Pounce and Pierce to lunge onto it and sink in his sharp fangs!

When prey scurry over the Goliath tarantula's silk threads, the vibration informs him that something is outside his burrow. If it's the likes of mice, frogs or the occasional bird, they're about to be this guy's dinner!

TRUE OR FALSE

Write either "true" or "false" next to each statement!

_____ **1.** The Goliath tarantula takes over another creature's burrow.

_____ **2.** The Goliath tarantula makes a trip wire from plant stems.

_____ **3.** The Goliath tarantula is a crustacean.

Answers on pg. 190

RED FOX

Found in forest patches, agricultural fields, shrubland and grassland, the den of a red fox serves many purposes. This red fox rests, gives birth and stores food in her burrow, and she also creates tunnels that lead to her favorite hunting areas above ground. When it's time to grab a fresh meal, the red fox uses her Creature Power of Fast Food Run to chase down the likes of rabbits, raccoons, squirrels and voles at speeds of 30 miles per hour or more!

When it comes to settling into a den, the red fox is resourceful. While she will often dig her own, she will sometimes modify the den of another animal or use a rock crevice or log pile to form a natural burrow.

FOX FINDER

Can you find seven red foxes hiding in this environment?

Answers on pg. 190

AARDWOLF

he may not have big muscles and claws like similar mammal species, but the aardwolf is still a skilled survivor! Abandoned springhare, porcupine and aardvark burrows often become the new home of the aardwolf, and she uses her burrow to rear and protect her young from threats such as the black-backed jackal. As an added measure to keep her cubs safe, she uses her Creature Power of On the Move, which is an anti-predation strategy that sees her moving her family to new den sites every so often!

MOVING DAY MAZE

Can you help the aardwolf move to a new den site to avoid predators?

END

Answer on pg. 190

During her active hours, the aardwolf is usually foraging for food. She particularly likes termites and can eat anywhere from 200 to 300,000 of them in a single night!

WARTHOG

This creature can be found sleeping or raising young in the abandoned burrows of animals such as aardvarks and porcupines, but she also uses the shelter to hide from predators such as lions, leopards and hyenas! While her sharp tusks can provide a powerful defense, sometimes she needs to get as far away from a threat as quickly as she can. When that happens, the warthog uses her Creature Power of Speedy Escape to run back to her burrow at speeds of about 34 miles per hour!

TUSK TASK

Find the warthogs with missing tusks, then draw them in. Once you're done, tally up the tusks you added!

_____ TUSKS

Answers on pg. 190

When the warthog is looking for a meal rather than watching out for a predator, she uses her incredible sense of smell to locate the likes of berries, grasses, bark, roots and the occasional worm and other bug. I can relate—I always let my nose lead the way to good food!

WOLVERINE

Meet the second-largest member of the weasel family! The wolverine is known for being an energetic creature with a very high metabolism, and she's clever when it comes to keeping herself fed. Thanks to her Creature Power of Ultra Travel, this mighty mammal can cover 30 miles in a day to find food! And if she ends up with any leftovers, she can hide them in snow, bogs or under boulders for later.

The wolverine also digs some pretty impressive burrows to sleep in. Using her muscular limbs and sturdy claws, she can build a burrow more than 30 feet deep and 164 feet in length!

WOLVERINE WORDS

Can you find these words relating to the wolverine?

BURROW
WEASEL
MAMMAL
CLAWS
ENERGETIC
TRAVEL
SNOW
BOGS
BOULDERS

Answers on pg. 190

```
E N L E G W K X R B
N C B V S J O C S U
E S Q W J X K L N R
R H H G E M R A O R
G M A M M A L W W O
E U X B M R S S L W
T H X O F U H E H C
I W B G J B Q W L T
C W Y S T R A V E L
H B O U L D E R S K
```

165

INDIAN CRESTED PORCUPINE

This nocturnal rodent puts his muscles and strong claws to good use! The Indian crested porcupine digs burrows that have a long entrance, a big main chamber and multiple exits. With his Creature Power of Super Senses, he can smell bulbs, roots and tubers underground or get a feel for his environment with the sensitive, stiff hairs surrounding his snout and eyes!

POINT OUT THE DIFFERENCE

Can you spot the five differences between these two images of the Indian crested porcupine?

Answers on pg. 190

He gets straight to the point!

I really "dig" this guy—and I definitely wouldn't want to mess with him! When faced with a threat, the Indian crested porcupine raises his quills and moves backward to lodge some in the attacker!

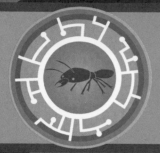

HARVESTER TERMITE

The harvester termite sure knows how to hide! This insect is a favorite food of the bat-eared fox but he uses his Creature Power of Deep Dig to build underground tunnel nests where he can safely store his food and feast with other harvester termites!

Wow, this tiny bug packs a lot of power!

He sure does, bro! Especially in his strong jaw, which allows him to cut through big blades of live and dead grass to chow down!

TERMITE MAZE

Can you find the tunnel that leads
to the harvester termite?

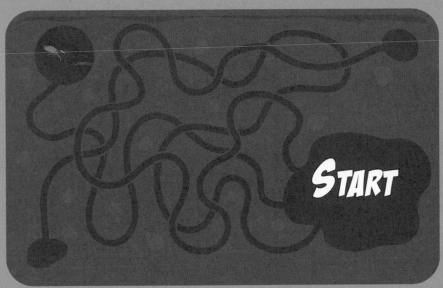

Start

Answer on pg. 191

BURROWING OWL

The burrowing owl is always prepared for danger! Using her claws and feet to kick out soil, this bird chooses to build her nest in areas with low-lying vegetation so she can spot any sneaky predators that might try to attack her and her nest. If she feels threatened while in her nest, the burrowing owl uses her Creature Power of Tricky Hiss to make a sound that can fool predators into thinking she's a rattlesnake!

SPOT THE DIFFERENCE

Can you find the five differences between these burrowing owls?

Answers on pg. 191

GREEN ANACONDA

Found in South America, this carnivorous creature makes great use of the ground below! When conditions get too hot and humid, the green anaconda will burrow into mud and remain very still until rain and moisture returns. And if he gets hungry, he can use his Creature Power of Food Vibrations to sense subtle movements made by approaching animals such as frogs, rodents, peccaries and deer!

Instead of burrowing in the mud, the green anaconda will sometimes slither into water to escape the heat. I like that option better— I'd much rather jump in a pool than a mud puddle on a hot day!

Ha, same!

SNAKE MAZE

Help the green anaconda slither his way to the water!

Answer on pg. 191

EARTHWORM

This wiggly creature is capable of some spectacular feats! The earthworm is great at keeping soil healthy and fertile, helping plants grow from the ground he lives in. And while he does have many predators, he has an incredible way of dealing with injuries: If his tail is cut off, the earthworm uses his **Creature Power of Miracle Heal** to grow a new one!

There's nothing small about the earthworm's appetite! A population of earthworms living in an acre of land can process over 9 tons (18,000 pounds!) of leaves, dirt, dead roots and stems per year!

What a feast!

WORMY WORDS

Unscramble these words relating to the earthworm!

ILOS_____

CRIMALE LEAH_____

RITD_____

NUOGRD_____

LPANST_____

JURNIISE_____

TPAEEPTI_____

Answers on pg. 191

ANSWER KEY

PG. 10 MENU MATCHING

1
Fish
Frogs
Spiders
Crustaceans

2
Fish
Birds
Turtles
Sandshrews

3
Fish
Crustaceans
Turtles
Birds

4
Fish
Scorpions
Leopard Seals
Turtles

PG. 4 SPY FROM THE SKY

PG. 7 GOOSE CROSSING

```
        ¹M
  ²F L I E S
  L     I
  O     L
  C   ³S O U T H
⁴B E A K
```

PG. 9 SQUIRREL SCRAMBLE

SERTEPTO = **TREETOPS**

UFYRR = **FURRY**

BMMEERAN = **MEMBRANE**

PTAAUIMG = **PATAGIUM**

LIGFNY = **FLYING**

IDGEL = **GLIDE**

PG. 12 HIDING BIRDS

PG. 14 SKY AND SEA SEARCH

```
O Z W Z P F Y S H P
F I L I Z L O W L L
S P R I N G T I M E
F L A P O G K M K B
C U H Y O K S R B I
U N D E R W A T E R
S W I M M I N G A D
M F U Z T M E F K X
X S E A P A R R O T
X W F L Y I N G S I
```

PG. 17 QUETZAL QUIZ

1. C. GREEN
2. A. SWALLOWING THEM WHOLE IN MIDAIR
3. D. TO ATTRACT A MATE
4. B. 3 FEET

PG. 19 EYE TO THE SKY

PG. 21 DRAGONFLY JUMBLE

GNSWI = <u>WINGS</u>

TINCES = <u>INSECT</u>

RAVLLA = <u>LARVAL</u>

TROPELIEHC = <u>HELICOPTER</u>

KXTOEEOESLN = <u>EXOSKELETON</u>

OREVH = <u>HOVER</u>

PG. 23 EYE TO THE SKY

PG. 25 SPOT THE DIFFERENCE

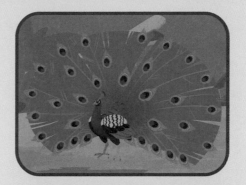

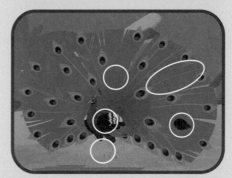

PG. 26 PREY WATCH

Answer Key

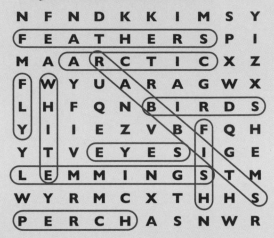

PG. 27 BIRD SEARCH

```
T W R I W G K C R M
W A S E O N Q O E J
P E C H O C B N G T
R O A T L H Y S G E
E F F V I G J P S A
Y O L N E C G I T M
J L B O B X S R C O
V M E G C G H A K R
N E S T J K S C S K
A O H M Q I M Y S K
```

PG. 29 MIGRATION MAZE

END

PG. 30 ODD OWL OUT

PG. 32 SNOWY SEARCH

```
N F N D K K I M S Y
F E A T H E R S P I
M A A R C T I C X Z
F W Y U A R A G W X
L H F Q N B I R D S
Y I I E Z V B F Q H
Y T V E Y E S I G E
L E M M I N G S T M
W Y R M C X T H H S
P E R C H A S N W R
```

PG. 35 JUMBLE BEE

OOLYCN = COLONY

ORRWKE = WORKER

IHEV = HIVE

LFY = FLY

OHYNE = HONEY

ZFYZU = FUZZY

WLEFRO = FLOWER

PG. 36 SUPERB BIRD WORDS

```
O I F E A T H E R S
C N E W G U I N E A
T R A N S F O R M S
H B C D C R O W N T
O L A Y A W V F A S
P U P M Z N E D K H
L E E C H J C K E J
R A I N F O R E S T
S J M A R K I N G S
I Y O A N O M J Q J
```

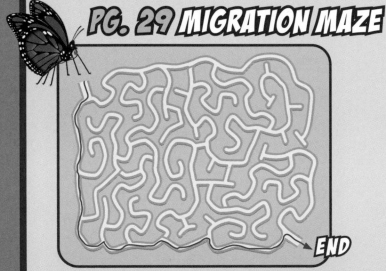

PG. 39 CROSSBIRD PUZZLE

PG. 45 ALL MIXED UP

GMERTAI = <u>MIGRATE</u>

LFY = <u>FLY</u>

ZBILRA = <u>BRAZIL</u>

ILBL = <u>BILL</u>

NNETSGI = <u>NESTING</u>

OSPWO = <u>SWOOP</u>

CSOPO = <u>SCOOP</u>

PG. 41 WASP WORDS

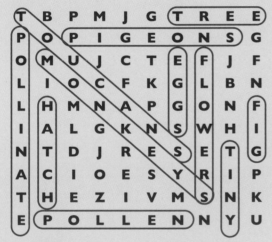

PG. 46 SPOT THE DIFFERENCE

PG. 43 SHADOW MATCHING

PG. 47 BIRDS OF A FEATHER

Answer Key

PG. 49 LIGHT THE WAY

END

PG. 51 HIDING SPOTS

PG. 53 JOLTED JUMBLE

DUWEERNRTA = <u>UNDERWATER</u>

CTELYCIIRTE = <u>ELECTRICITY</u>

LSCEL = <u>CELLS</u>

TNSU = <u>STUN</u>

SFHI = <u>FISH</u>

GROFS = <u>FROGS</u>

OKHSC VEAW = <u>SHOCK WAVE</u>

PG. 55 SWIM TO SAFETY

PG. 57 FISHIN' FOR WORDS

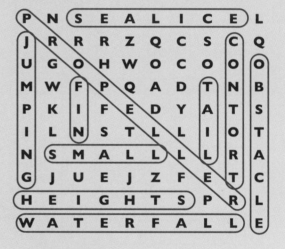

PG. 59 FOLLOW THE SOUND

PG. 61 OTTER SPOTTING

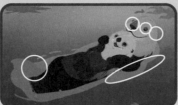

PG. 63 DEEP-SEA SEARCH

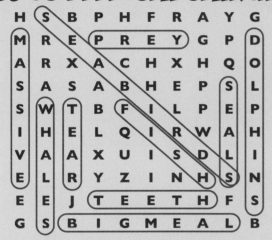

PG. 65 ALL JUM-BULLED UP

DOTERPAR = PREDATOR

WMSI = SWIM

ANCEO = OCEAN

UPPS = PUPS

SSNATIEDC = DISTANCES

UTESSRAIE = ESTUARIES

VIRRSE = RIVERS

PG. 66 UNDERWATER MAZE

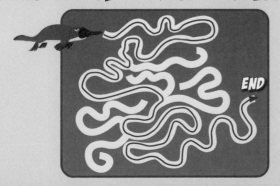

PG. 69 SEA SCRAMBLE

YIPNS = SPINY

LEHLS = SHELL

ESA TORTES = SEA OTTERS

LSEE = EELS

SLUSMES = MUSSELS

LEKP = KELP

LHIMECAC = CHEMICAL

PG. 71 FISHIN' FOR WORDS

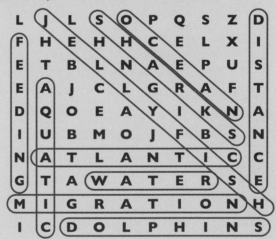

PG. 73 KRILL IN THE BLANKS

1. DESCENDS
2. 140 FEET
3. DIGESTING
4. MIGRATES
5. SURFACE
6. GRAZE
7. FEEDING HABITS
8. PREDATORS

Answer Key

PG. 78 MANTA MAZE

PG. 74 FLOUNDER FINDER

PG. 80 SNAPPER SEARCH

```
S  T  L  Z  F  J  I  J  E  J
W  N  N  P  L  A  N  K  T  O  N
W  S  A  O  C  E  P  E  L  E  C
W  O  Z  H  P  C  D  N  E  L  A
R  O  R  S  Q  R  A  T  R  T  E  N
M  M  X  Q  H  I  C  O  H  Y  I
S  C  S  U  J  M  T  P  F  N
D  R  W  E  I  J  P  I  U  E
S  A  B  Z  K  Z  D  T  M  O  S
Z  B  C  H  O  W  D  O  W  N
```

PG. 75 TRUE OR FALSE

1. TRUE
2. FALSE
3. FALSE
4. TRUE
5. FALSE

PG. 77 SPOT THE DIFFERENCE

PG. 83 SPOT THE DIFFERENCE

PG. 84 TUSK TASK

5 TUSKS

PG. 86 SEA SEARCH

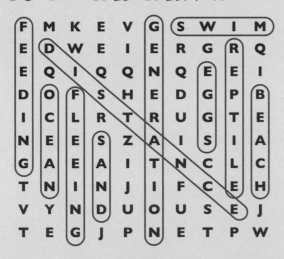

PG. 89 SNACK SEEKER

PG. 91 APE MAZE

PG. 93 LIFT OR LEAVE?

48 MG LEAVE   30 MG LIFT

26 MG LIFT   36 MG LEAVE

28 MG LIFT   31 MG LIFT

PG. 95 WILDCAT WORDS

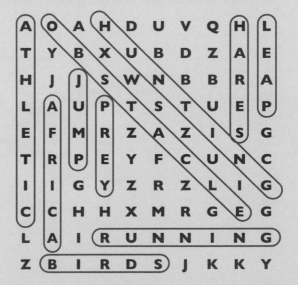

ANSWER KEY

PG. 97 SCRAMBLED SOUNDS

FOLW   W O L F

CAOVL   V O C A L

DOMO   M O O D

WROLG   G R O W L

SIGNATURE: Hoooooowl!

PG. 99 MANE EVENT

PG. 101 FOSSA WORD FINDER

```
F A M B A N K L E S
N L C A R Z A Z G V
N E P L M U L P S C
N M P R A I M C S O L
F U R E N O M A K Z A
P R E D C C T B L S W
R S A E J Q A I N S
E E T H E Q J I N J
Y R O T Y D X D L G
U U R A J T R E E S
```

PG. 103 MAKING A MARK

END

PG. 105 SPOT THE DIFFERENCE

PG. 107 WILD WORDS

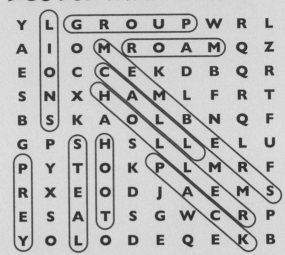

PG. 113 MATCHING STRIPES

PG. 109 WHERE'D THE GECKO GO?

PG. 115 MONKEY JUMBLE

SERET	=	TREES
HOATTR	=	THROAT
MECSAR	=	SCREAM
DUSTLEO	=	LOUDEST
CVEIO	=	VOICE
MULEVO	=	VOLUME
DWORY RRAO	=	ROWDY ROAR

PG. 116 HIDING HEDGEHOGS

PG. 111 RUMBLE JUMBLE

LMMMAA	=	MAMMAL
BLUMRING	=	RUMBLING
RHDE	=	HERD
REQFUEYCN	=	FREQUENCY
NSSDUO	=	SOUNDS
WDNA	=	DAWN
USDK	=	DUSK

ANSWER KEY

PG. 117 SPOT THE DEER-FERENCE

PG. 119 BIRD WORD FINDER

F	S	G	N	I	W	U	U	T
A	E	Y	V	A	K	U	H	R
S	K	P	X	E	G	G	S	U
T	H	Z	A	N	O	S	S	N
E	B	Z	Z	C	P	K	E	N
S	Z	G	S	M	S	I	W	I
T	Q	G	E	W	W	E	U	N
W	E	C	U	Q	P	D	P	G
L	I	D	H	W	R	X	Q	O

PG. 121 SPOT THE DIFFERENCE

PG. 123 COBRA CROSSWORD

¹FANGS
²PREDATOR
³FLEEING ⁴INSECT
⁵MAMMALS
⁶AFRIC
⁷BIRD
⁸SCALES
⁹SNAKES

PG. 125 KOALA TERMS

A	C	G	R	O	O	M	I	N	G
I	U	L	K	R	B	T	O	Z	F
T	B	S	A	V	P	S	Z	C	O
H	E	R	T	W	F	W	L	L	R
U	A	X	A	R	H	S	D	I	A
M	T	E	P	N	A	O	B	M	G
B	I	K	A	X	C	L	O	B	I
P	N	R	W	Z	M	H	I	K	N
C	G	W	S	A	P	E	E	A	G
S	L	E	E	P	I	N	G	S	I

186

PG. 127 BAMBOOZLED!

OBOMAB = <u>BAMBOO</u>

ALMAMM = <u>MAMMAL</u>

VEELAS = <u>LEAVES</u>

EMSTS = <u>STEMS</u>

TEBI RECFO = <u>BITE FORCE</u>

CLUSEM OHMTU = <u>MUSCLE MOUTH</u>

NLATP = <u>PLANT</u>

PG. 129 TALL TERMS

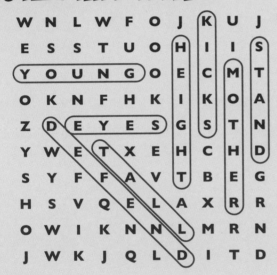

PG. 131 ERMINE MAZE

PG. 133 DRAGON JUMBLE

ZIRDLA = <u>LIZARD</u>

ALTI HPWI = <u>TAIL WHIP</u>

LWSCA = <u>CLAWS</u>

ERPY = <u>PREY</u>

ETHET = <u>TEETH</u>

REDE = <u>DEER</u>

GPI = <u>PIG</u>

CSUULRAM = <u>MUSCULAR</u>

PG. 134 CLIMB AND CLAIM

PG. 135 LOOK-ALIKE LIZARDS

ANSWER KEY

PG. 137 CREATURE CROSSWORD

Crossword grid:
- 3 across: BURROW
- 1 down: INSECTS
- 2 down: CLAWS
- 4 down: SMELL
- 5 across: TERMITES
- 5 down: TONGUE
- 6 across: SNOUT

PG. 143 TENREC TERMS

```
T U Q S R P X A T O
B O H U O P A P T B
S C B E I F Q Q T X
N K W L A L P S E Y
A I A D A D L H E T
K G W D I C B S T Y
E A K M D G K U H C
S W C R B Q Z I T T
M O N G O O S E S T
W V E J Y E L L O W
```

Words found: SNAKES, TEETH, MONGOOSES, YELLOW

PG. 139 ODD OTTER OUT

PG. 141 CREATURE QUIZ

1. B. NOUNS, VERBS, ADJECTIVES
2. C. COLONY
3. A. NESTING AND NURSING
4. C. ALL OF THE ABOVE

PG. 145 CLAM SCRAMBLE

ELHLS = SHELL
OFTO = FOOT
ADNS = SAND
NROCAH = ANCHOR
EATRW = WATER
SABCR = CRABS
RIFSHSAT = STARFISH
LULSG = GULLS

PG. 147 DIGGING FOR WORDS

```
Q B H K C A N I N E
T U X B E B S B V N
I S L E O B W U I E
P B T C W X I R W L
L R F J X Y M R L C
Q Y E I V F X O E N
D R D Y E J F W W D
I P G K Y K Y S Z I
G B W E B B E D F R
A R M A D I L L O T
```

PG. 149 ODD ONE OUT

PG. 151 ALL JUMBLED UP

TREESD = <u>DESERT</u>
ACMO = <u>CAMO</u>
EWTRA = <u>WATER</u>
NSAD = <u>SAND</u>
ETEF = <u>FEET</u>
DRSBI = <u>BIRDS</u>
ZIRDLAS = <u>LIZARDS</u>
GBUS <u>BUGS</u>

PG. 153 ALLIGATOR LOCATOR

PG. 155 TONGUE-TASTIC TERMS

```
L E E C L A W S T A
V M X M T O N G U E
L O Y D S N C S J H
H U U X A M M Y A M
U N V A F N E W Z X
V D E G C B T L Y R
B S T O L E C S L M
T E R M I T E S R Z
H E A R I N G Q J O
V I B R A T I O N S
```

PG. 157 SPOT THE DIFFERENCE

Answer Key

PG. 158 TRUE OR FALSE

1. TRUE
2. FALSE
3. FALSE

PG. 159 FOX FINDER

PG. 161 MOVING DAY MAZE

PG. 163 TUSK TASK

3 TUSKS

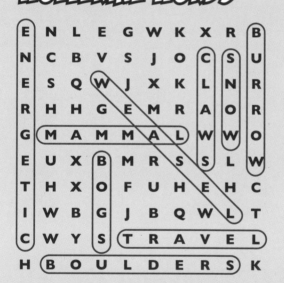

PG. 165 WOLVERINE WORDS

PG. 167 POINT OUT THE DIFFERENCE

PG. 169 TERMITE MAZE

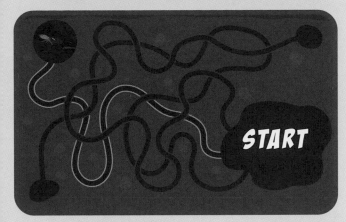

START

PG. 173 SNAKE MAZE

PG. 170 SPOT THE DIFFERENCE

PG. 175 WORMY WORDS

ILOS	=	SOIL
CRIMALE LEAH	=	MIRACLE HEAL
RITD	=	DIRT
NUOGRD	=	GROUND
LPANST	=	PLANTS
JURNIISE	=	INJURIES
TPAEEPTI	=	APPETITE

Media Lab Books
For inquiries, contact customerservice@topixmedia.com

Copyright 2024 Topix Media Lab

Published by Topix Media Lab
14 Wall Street, Suite 3C
New York, NY 10005

PRINTED IN CHINA

ISBN-13: 978-1-956403-75-6
ISBN-10: 1-956403-75-2

CEO Tony Romando

Vice President & Publisher Phil Sexton
Senior Vice President of Sales & New Markets Tom Mifsud
Vice President of Retail Sales & Logistics Linda Greenblatt
Vice President of Manufacturing & Distribution Nancy Puskuldjian
Digital Marketing & Strategy Manager Elyse Gregov

Chief Content Officer Jeff Ashworth
Senior Acquisitions Editor Noreen Henson
Creative Director Susan Dazzo
Photo Director Dave Weiss
Executive Editor Tim Baker
Managing Editor Tara Sherman

Content Editor Trevor Courneen
Associate Editor Juliana Sharaf
Designers Glen Karpowich, Alyssa Bredin Quirós, Mikio Sakai
Copy Editor & Fact Checker Madeline Raynor
Assistant Photo Editor Jenna Addesso
Assistant Managing Editor Claudia Acevedo

Topix Media Lab would like to thank the following Wild Kratts team members for their help in creating this publication:
Licensing Director Kaitlin Dupuis
Senior Researcher Deanna Ellis
Art Director Darren Ward

Photo Credits: 4-5 Twentytwo/Bigstock; 7, 13, 24, 38-39, 50-51, 63, 112, 124, 135 Shutterstock; 8, 42-43 Stephen Dalton/Minden Pictures; 10-11 Volodymyr Burdiak/AdobeStock; 14 Nature Photographers Ltd/Alamy; 16 Dennis Atencio/Alamy; 19 Steve Gettle/Minden Pictures; 20-21 Geoff Smith/Alamy; 23, 26, 48 Nature Picture Library/Alamy; 27 Tom Vezo/Minden Pictures; 29 Jerry and Marcy Monkman/EcoPhotography.com/Alamy; 31 Terry Sohl/Alamy; 33 jimkruger/iStock; 34-35 Michael Durham/Minden Pictures; 37, 105 Konrad Wothe/NPL/Minden Pictures; 41 Mark Moffett/Minden Pictures; 45, 75, 98 blickwinkel/Alamy; 46 Rolf Nussbaumer/NPL/Minden Pictures; 47 Rosanne Tackaberry/Alamy; 52 Gaertner/Alamy; 54 Prisma by Dukas Presseagentur GmbH/Alamy; 57 Matthias Breiter/Minden Pictures; 59 Kelvin Aitken/VWPics/Alamy; 61 Jody J. Overstreet/AdobeStock; 64 Pete Oxford/Minden Pictures; 66 D. Parer and E. Parer-Cook/Minden Pictures; 68-69 Fred Bavendam/Minden Pictures; 70 WaterFrame/Alamy; 73 David Tipling/NPL/Minden Pictures; 74 Pete Niesen/Alamy; 76 ephotocorp/Alamy; 79 Jordi Chias/NPL/Minden Pictures; 81 Tobias Bernhard Raff/Biosphoto/Minden Pictures; 82 Chase Dekker/Minden Pictures; 85 Galaxiid/Alamy; 86-87 Jon/AdobeStock; 89 Doug Perrine/Alamy; 91 Rolf Nussbaumer Photography/Alamy; 92 Kevin Wells/Alamy; 94-95, 102 Ann and Steve Toon/NPL/Minden Pictures; 96 Ben Queenborough/Alamy; 100 Chien Lee/Minden Pictures; 107, 122-123, 172-173 Nature Picture Library/Alamy; 108-109 Buiten-Beeld/Alamy; 110 Jon Arnold Images Ltd/Alamy; 115 Thomas Marent/Minden Pictures; 116, 154 imageBROKER/Alamy; 117 Andre Gilden/Alamy; 118 Mark Dumbleton/NiS/Minden Pictures; 121 Sylvain Cordier/Biosphoto/Minden Pictures; 126 Juergen and Christine Sohns/Minden Pictures; 128 Lori Ellis/Alamy; 130-131 Frederic Desmette/Biosphoto/Minden Pictures; 132 Kjersti Joergensen/Alamy; 134 All Canada Photos/Alamy; 136-137 Martin Harvey/Alamy Stock Photo; 138 Michael Quinton/Minden Pictures; 140 Donald M. Jones/Minden Pictures; 142 Arto Hakola/Alamy; 144 Martin Smart/Alamy; 146 Lauren Bilboe/Alamy; 148 Anton Sorokin/Alamy; 151 Gertrud && Helmut Denzau/NPL/Minden Pictures; 152 Heidi and Hans-Juergen Koch/Minden Pictures; 156 AGAMI Photo Agency/Alamy; 158 Piotr Naskrecki/Minden Pictures; 159 George Sanker/NPL/Minden Pictures; 160 Marco Valentini/Alamy; 162 photostaud/Alamy; 163-164 Robin Eriksson/Alamy; 166 Dave Watts/Alamy; 169 Vincent Grafhorst/Minden Pictures; 170 Tom Vezo/Minden Pictures; 175 Colin Varndell/Alamy